Art of the Protest

Words of Protest to color

Hey all! This is the beginning of a series of coloring books that have a use!

Art of the Protest is the first. This coloring book is meant to be colored for meditation and relaxation and then possibly used (if you so desire) to make signs.

Because the idea is to use the book I purposely made all the word doodles inside the lettering. I put one word per page so the words would be large enough and easy to cut out.

Also check out and post your own coloring pages to my Facebook page **Art of the Protest** and see how others used coloring pages to show their outrage. And remember…..

Indignation calls for pigmentation!

Let's color our way to a world where everyone has a seat at the table.

K.J.Givens

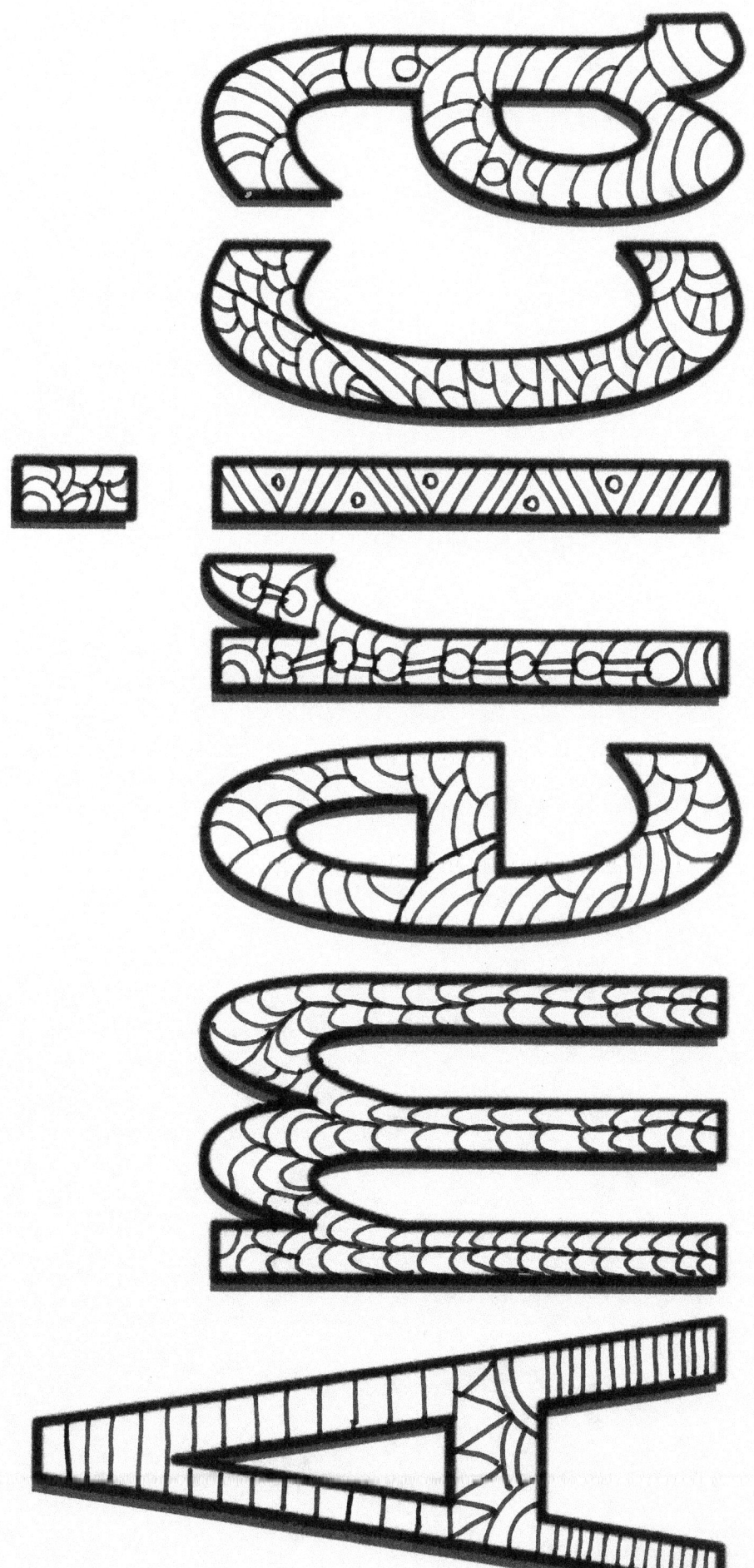

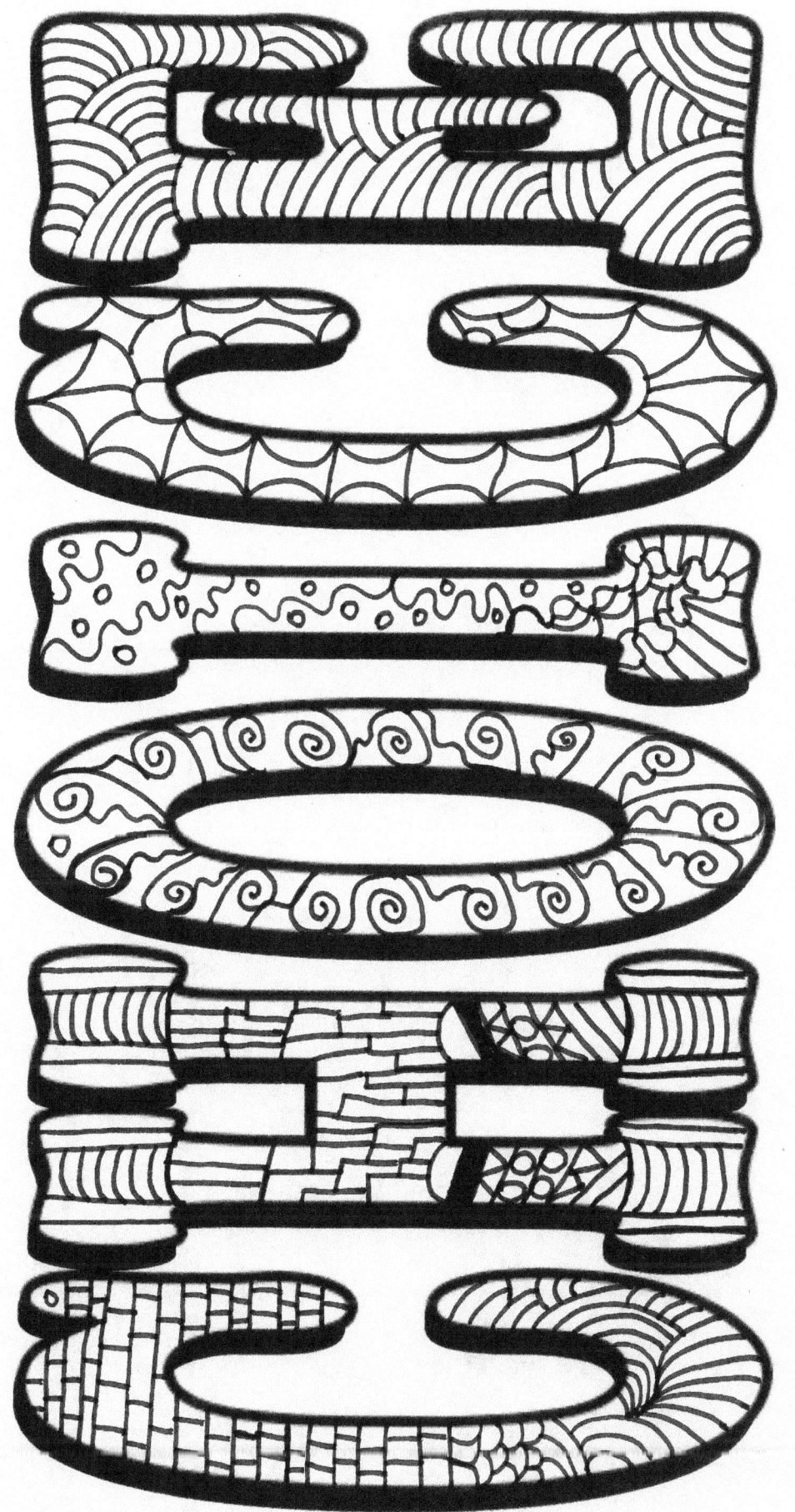

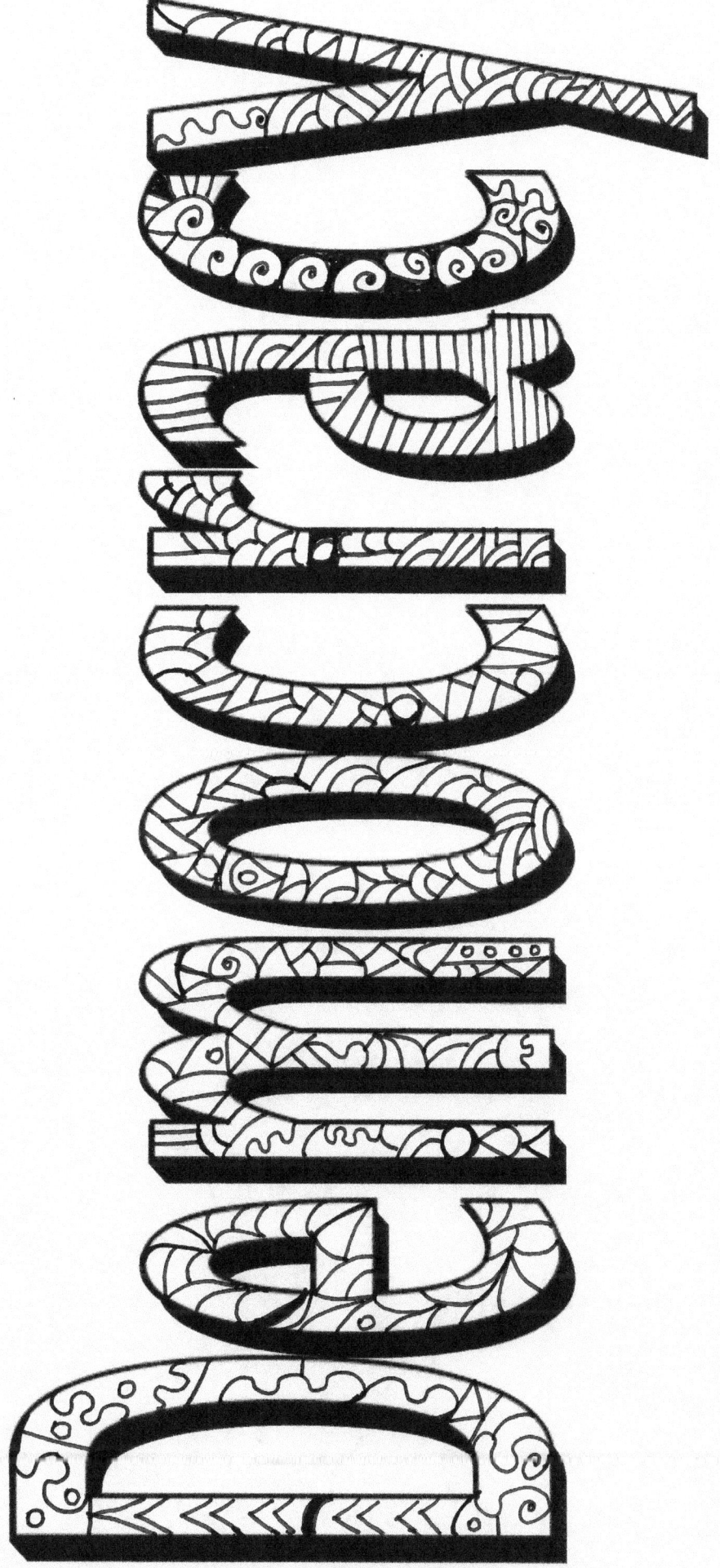

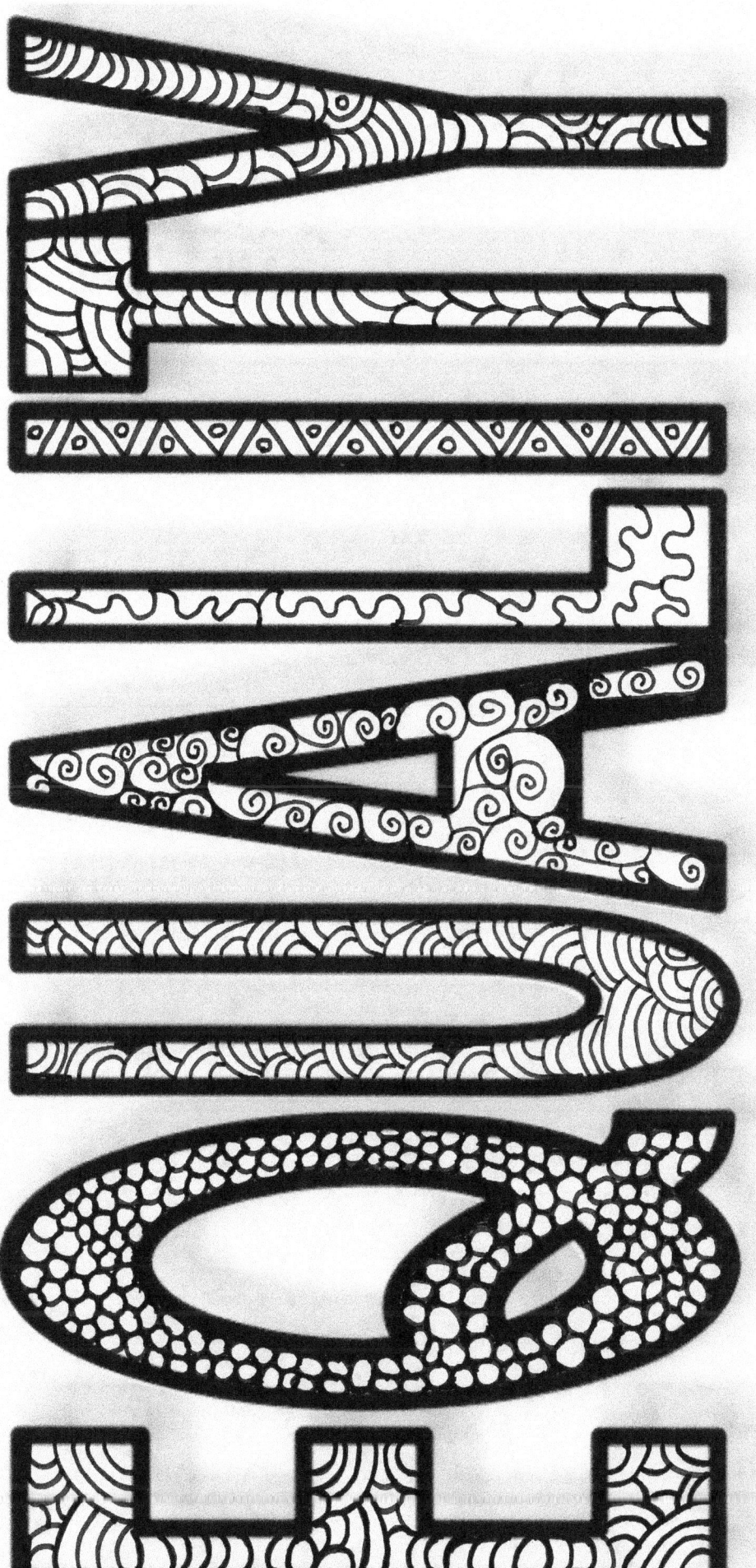

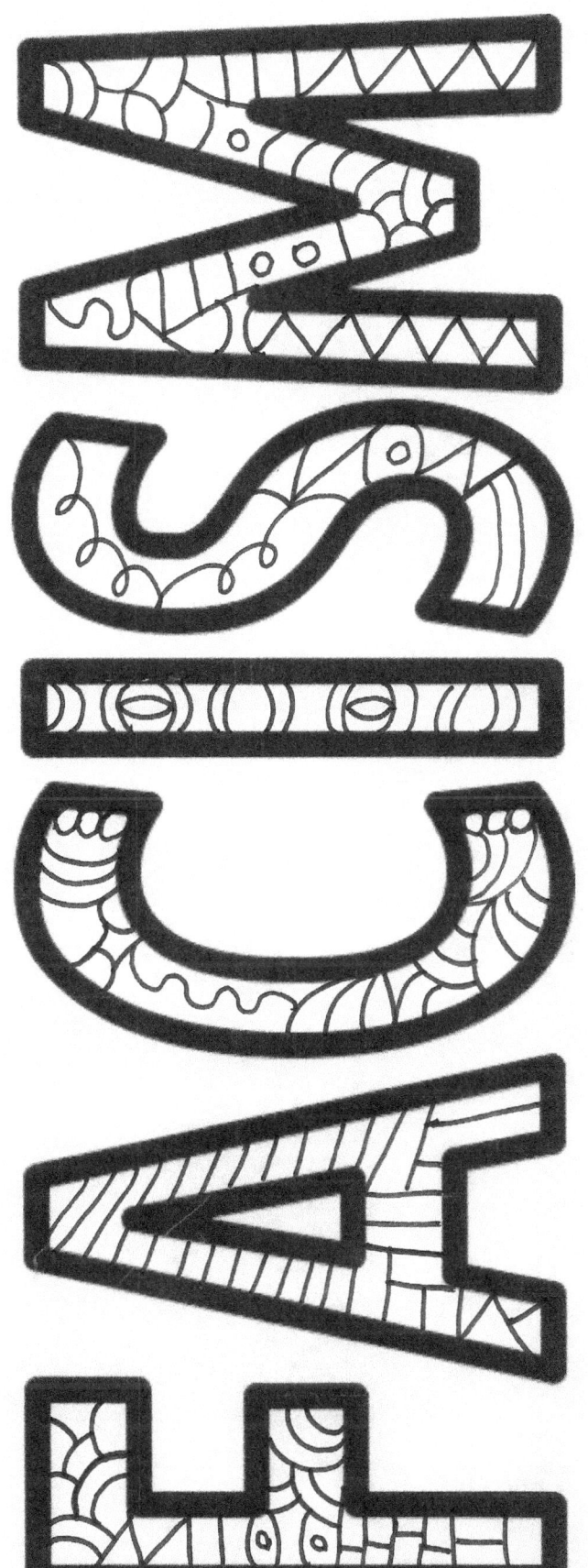

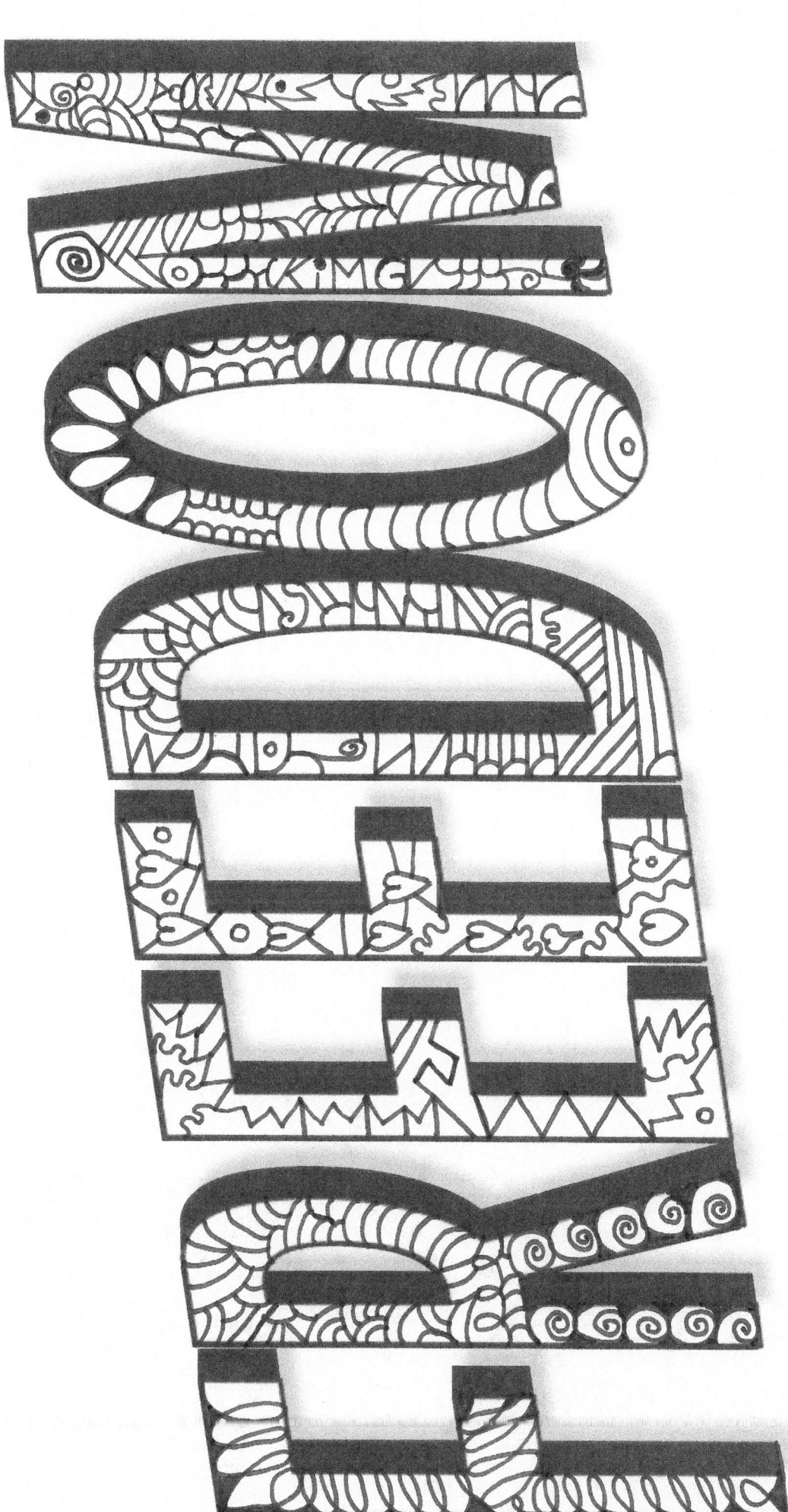

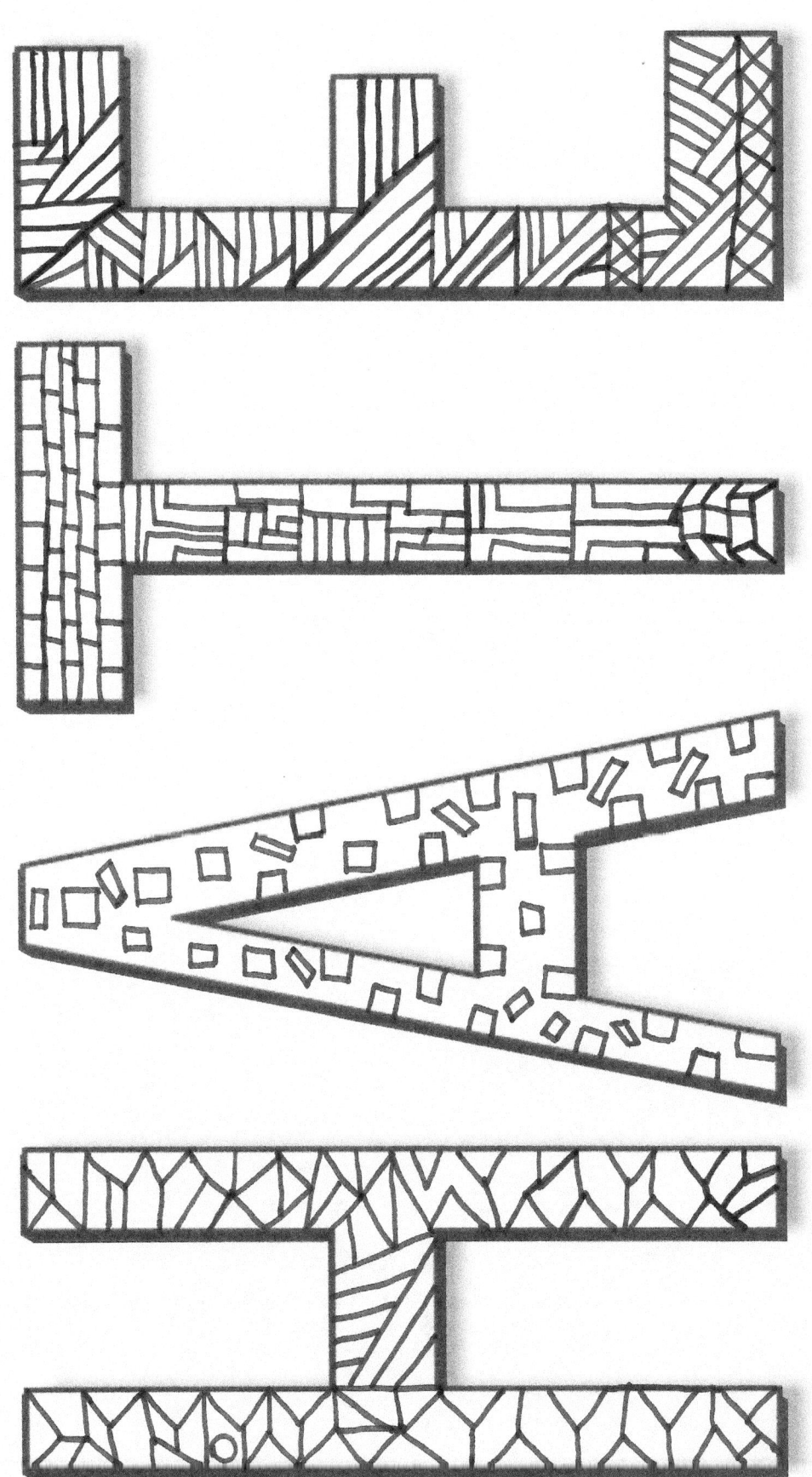

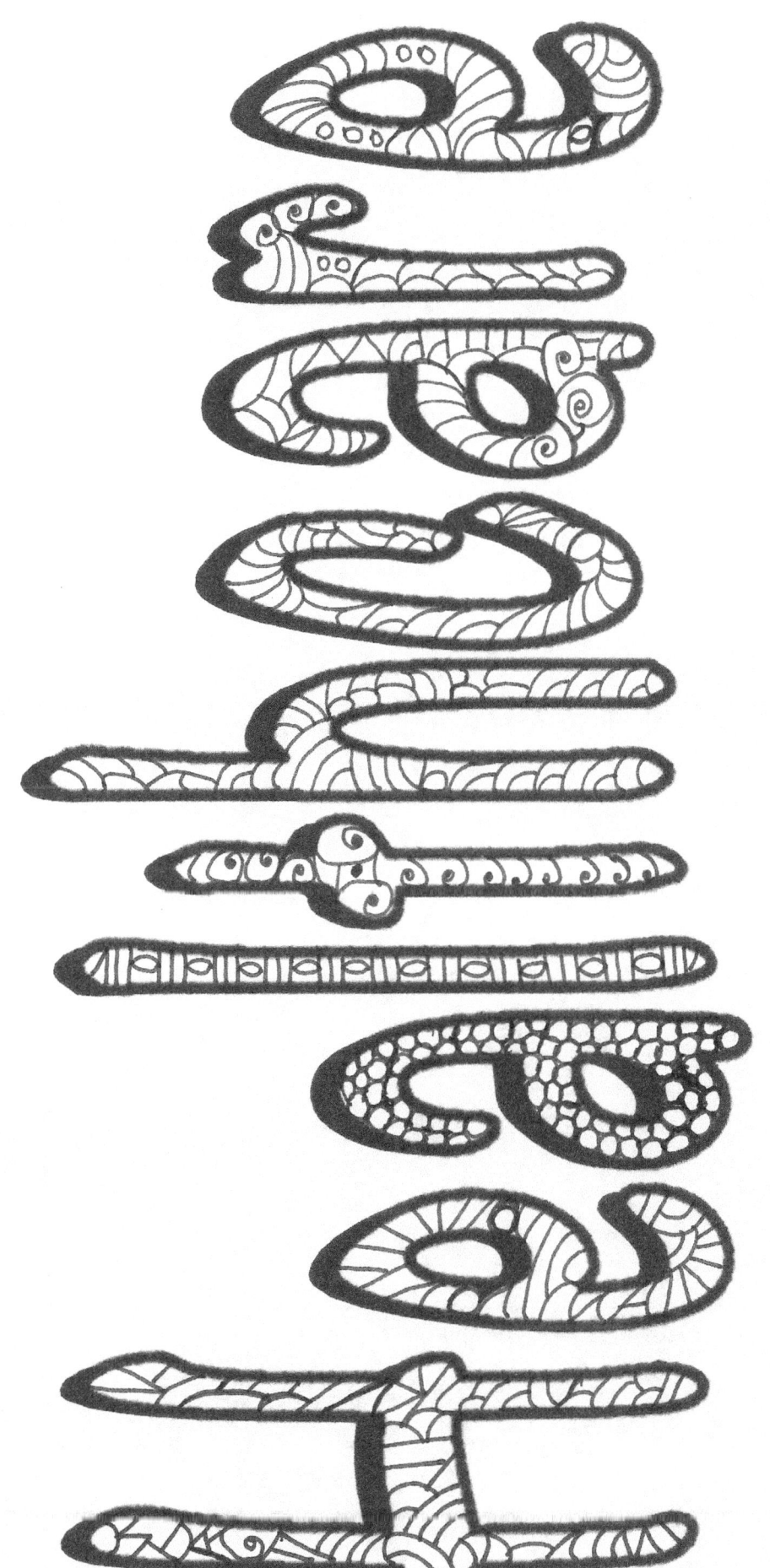

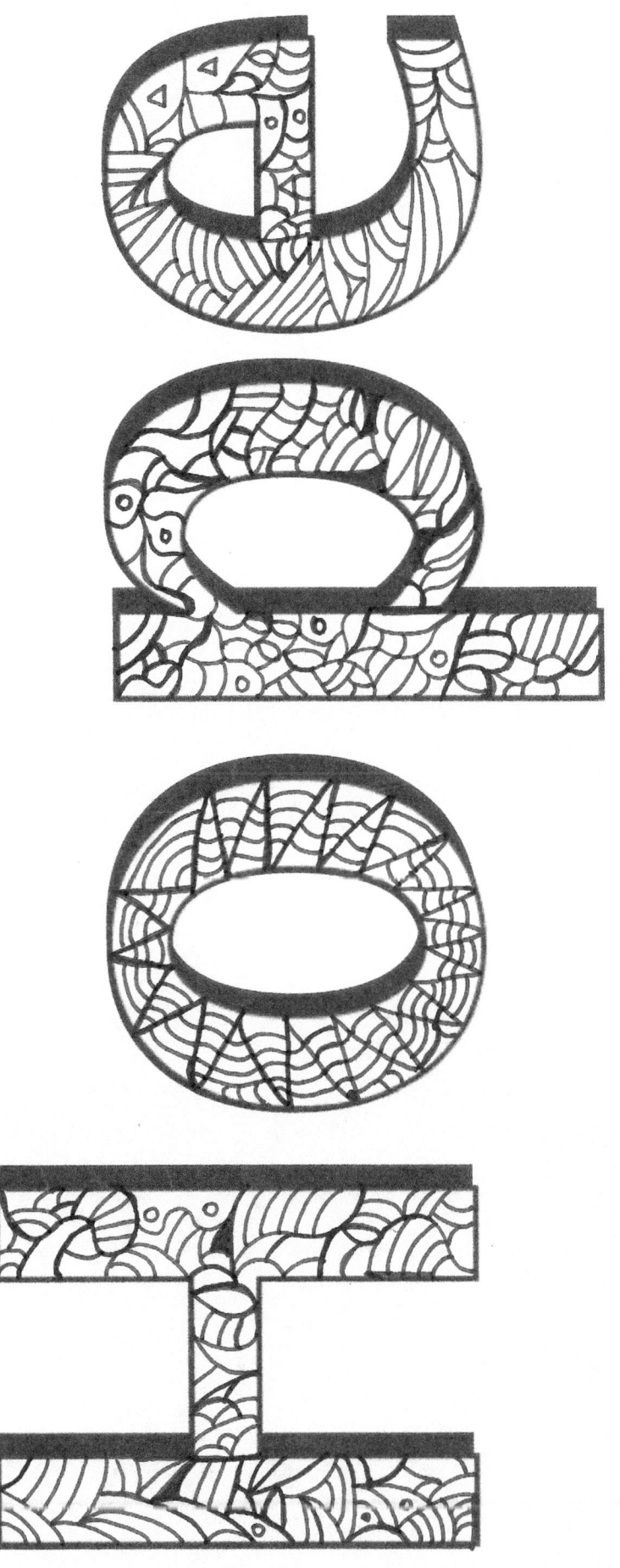

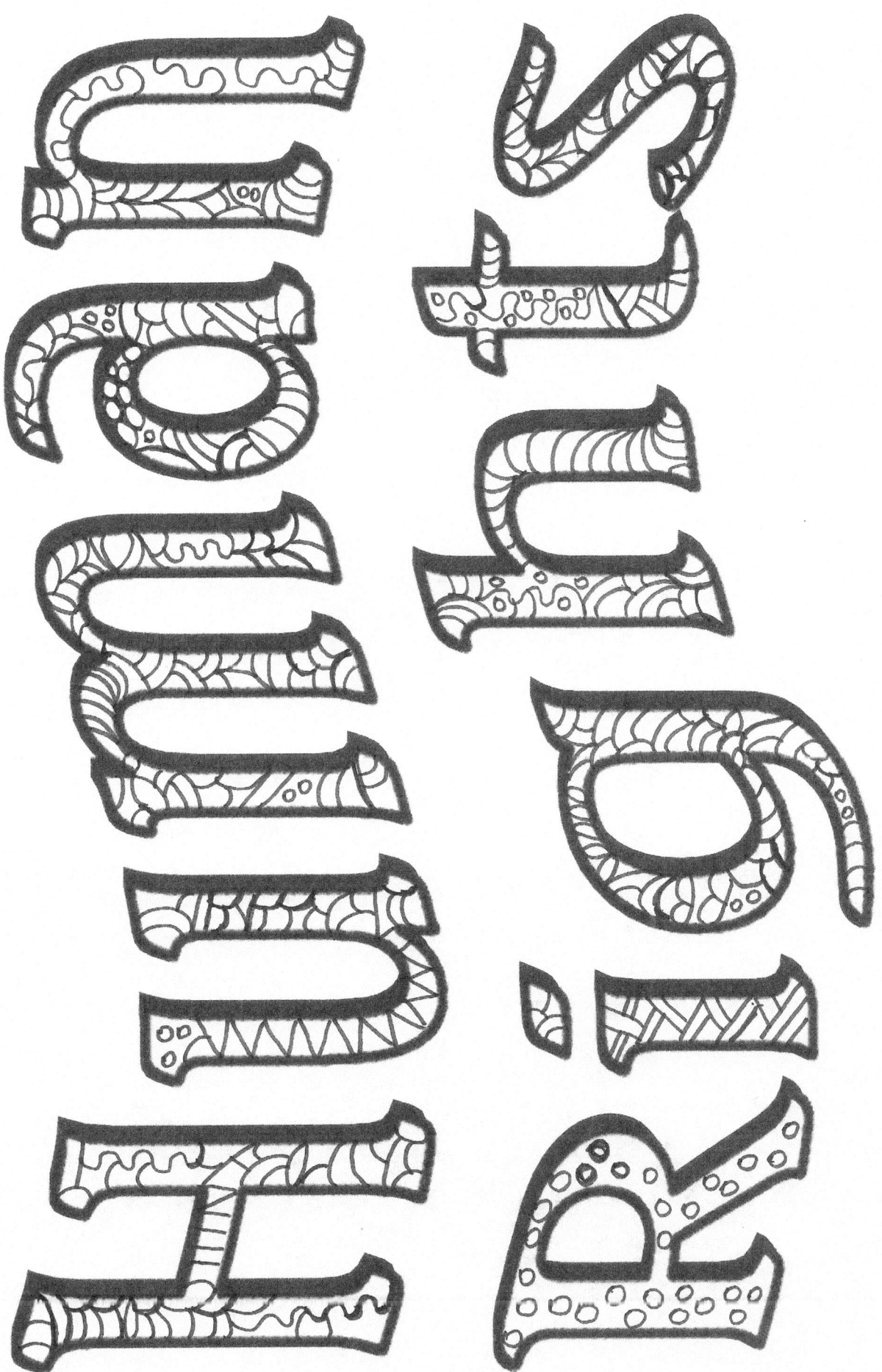

What's right humans FAR

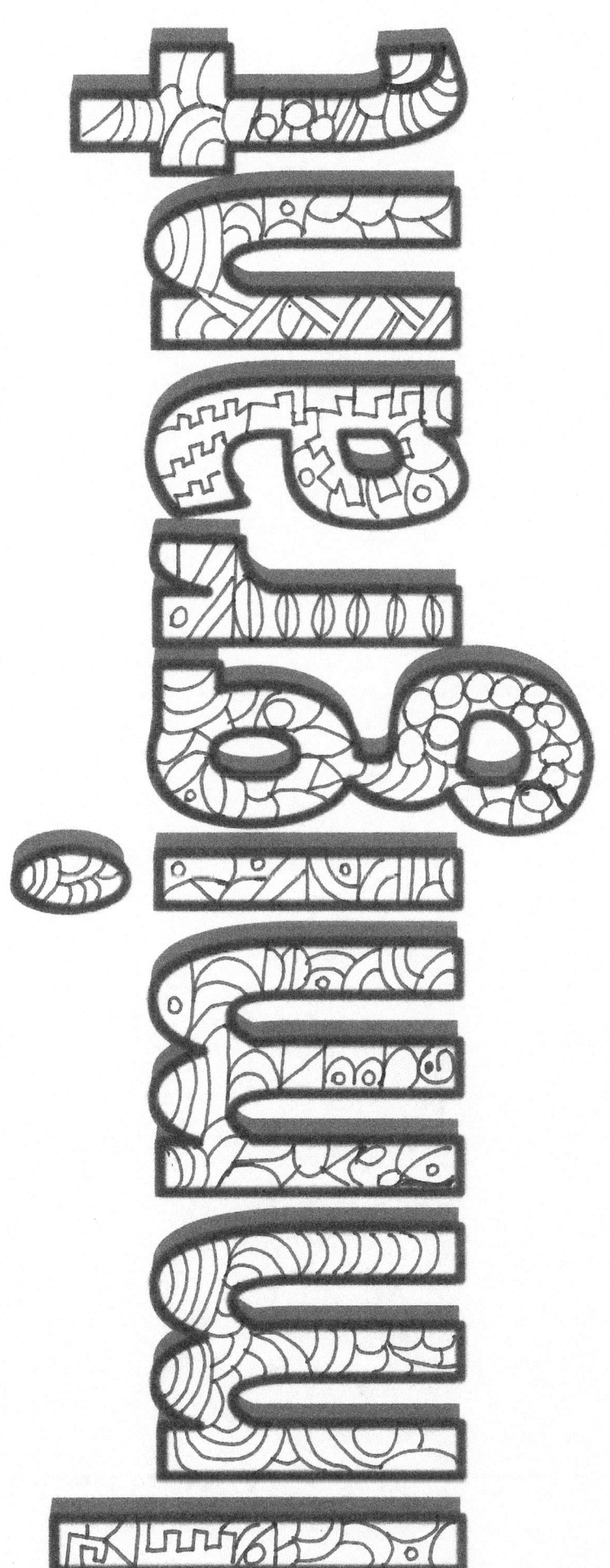

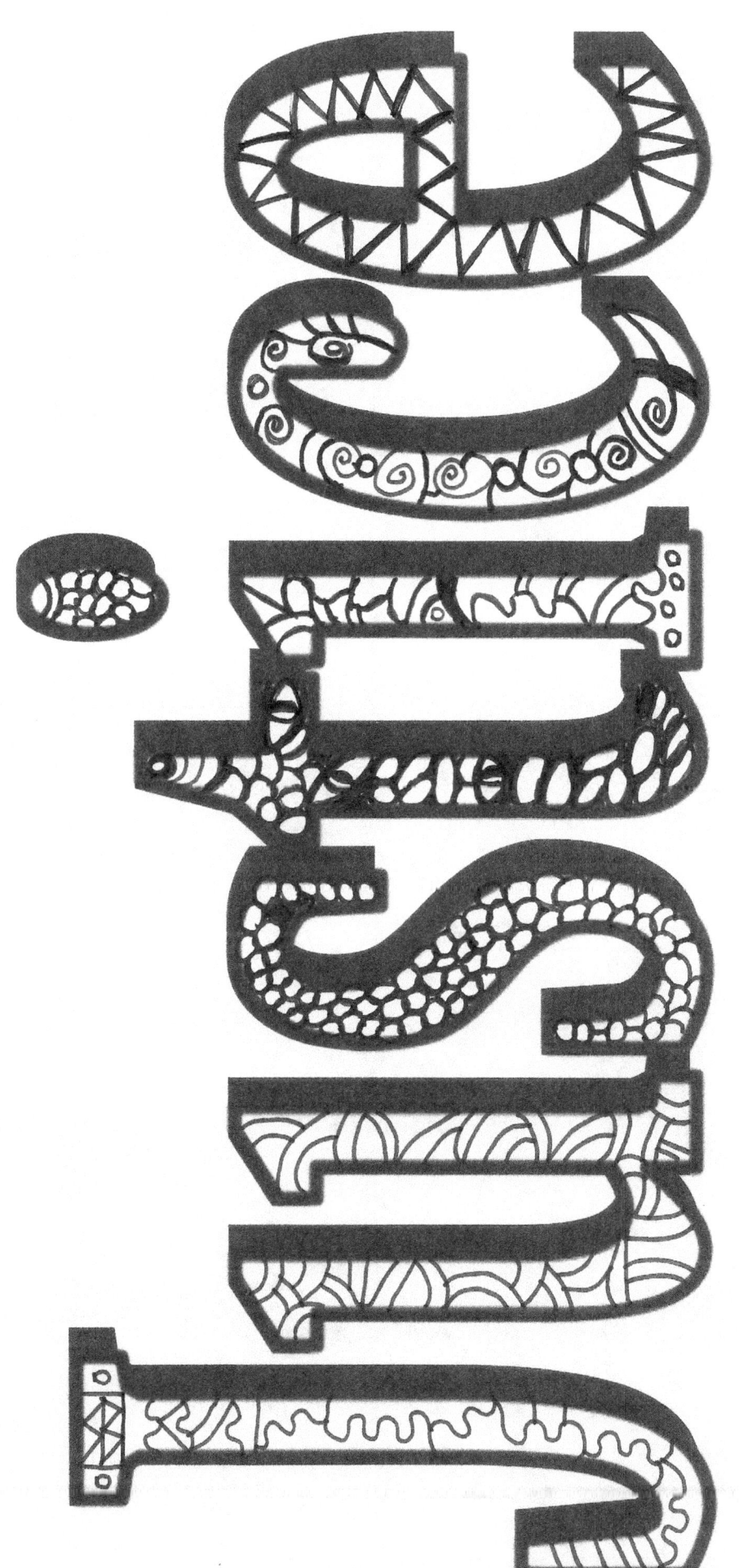

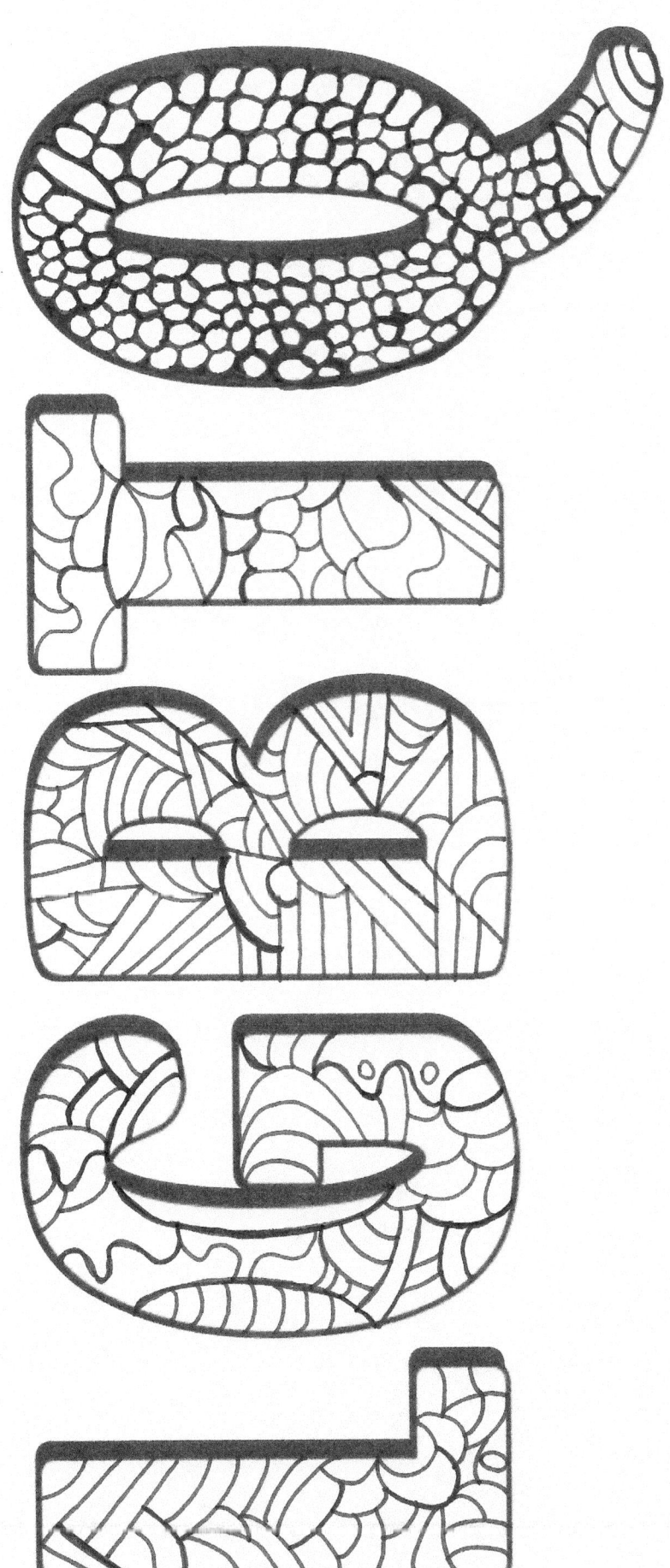

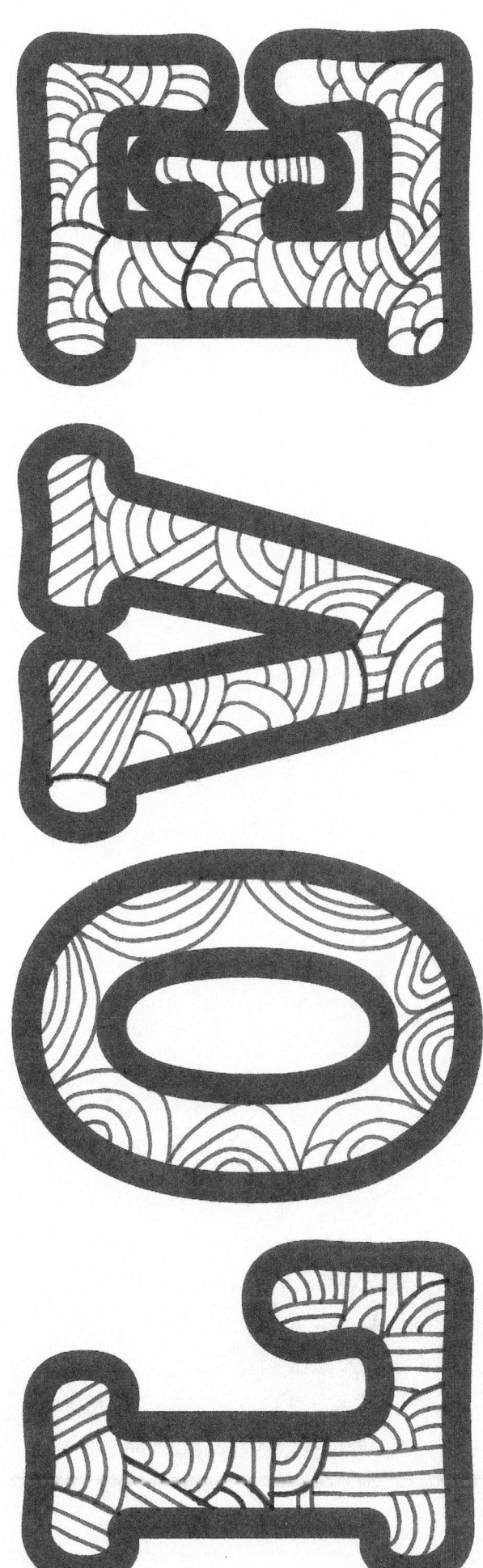

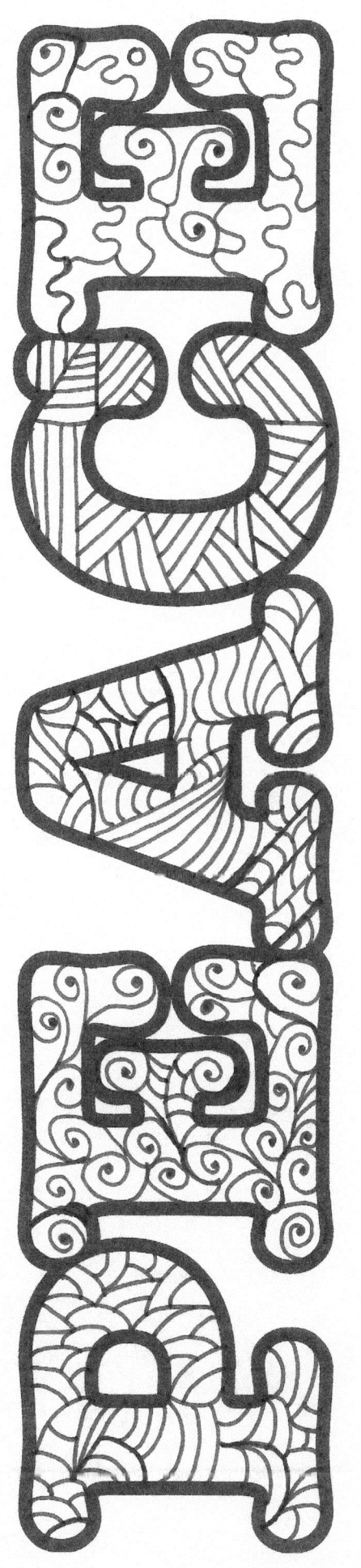

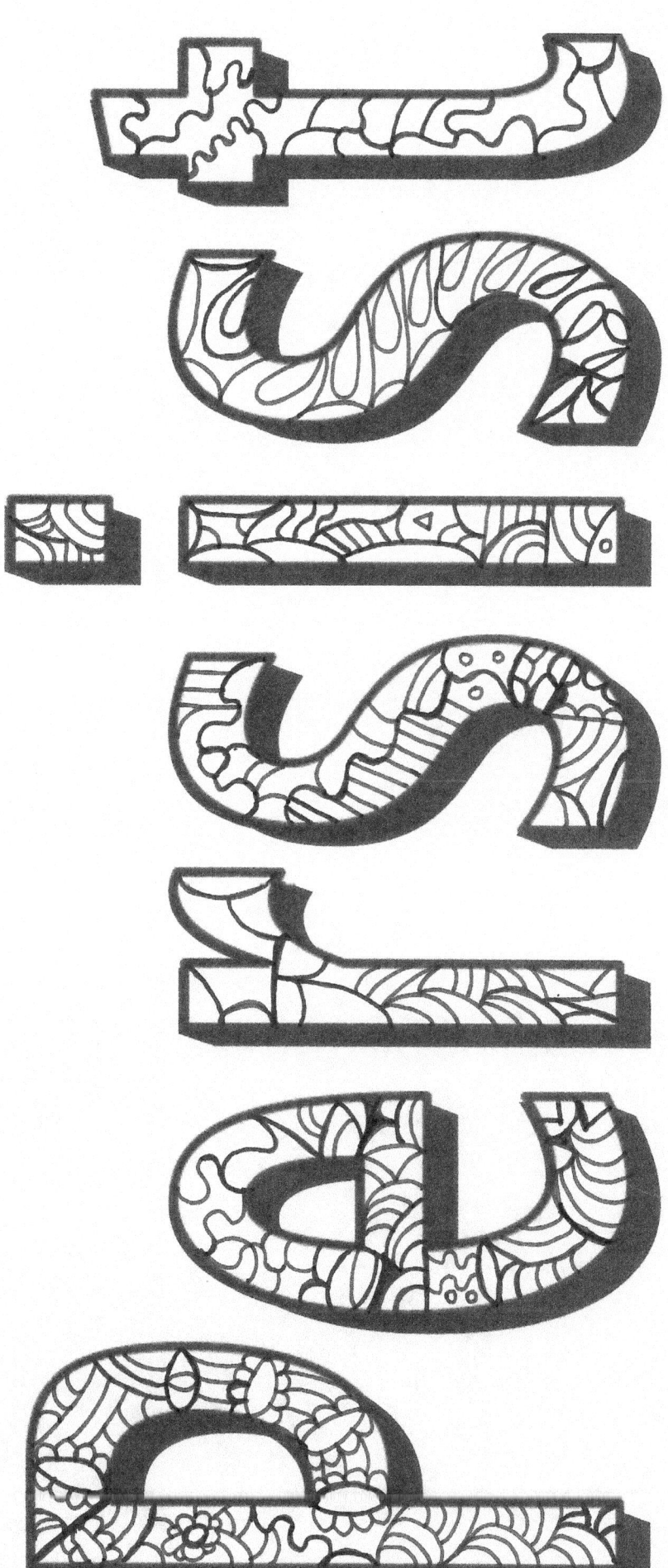

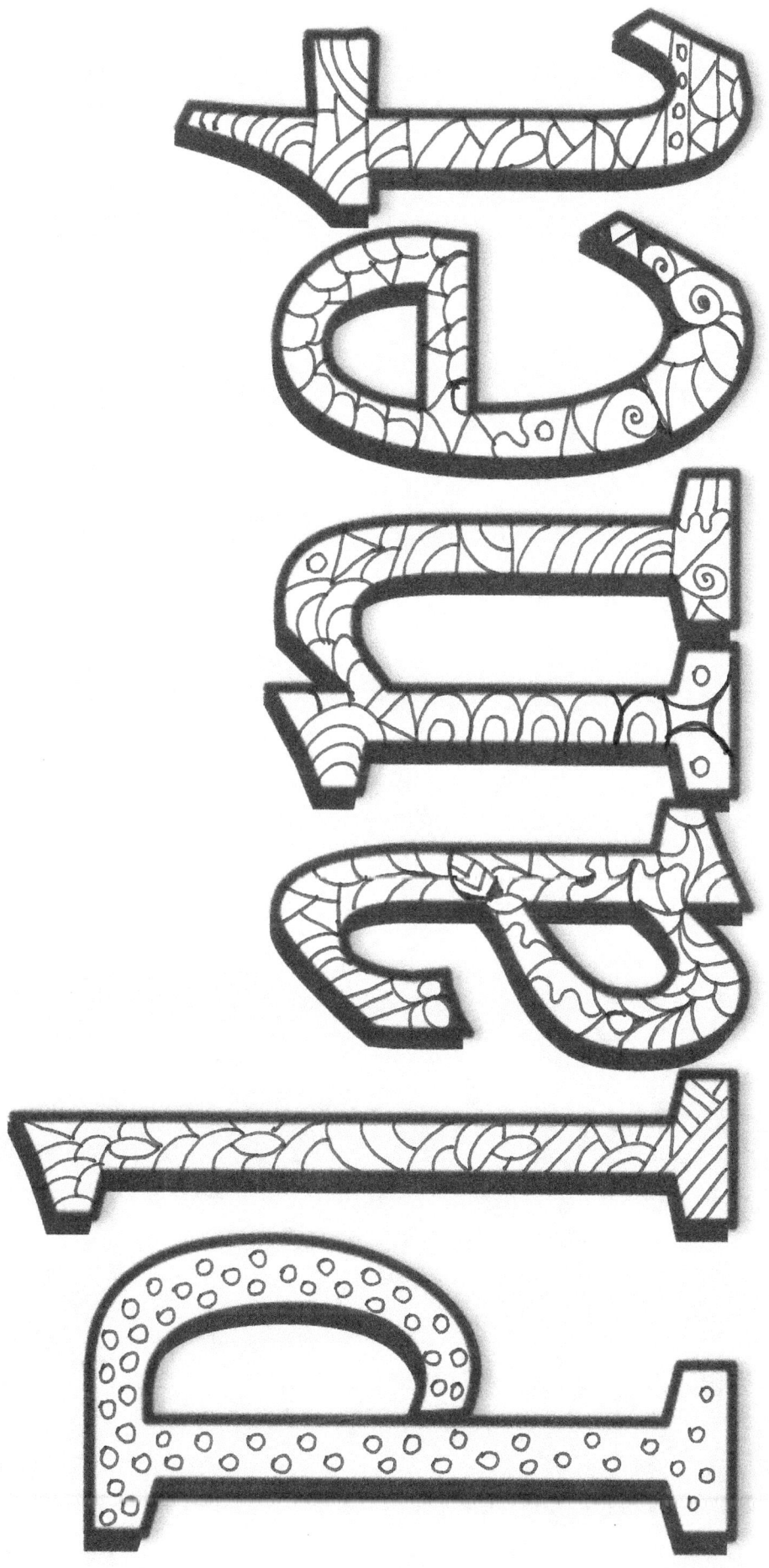

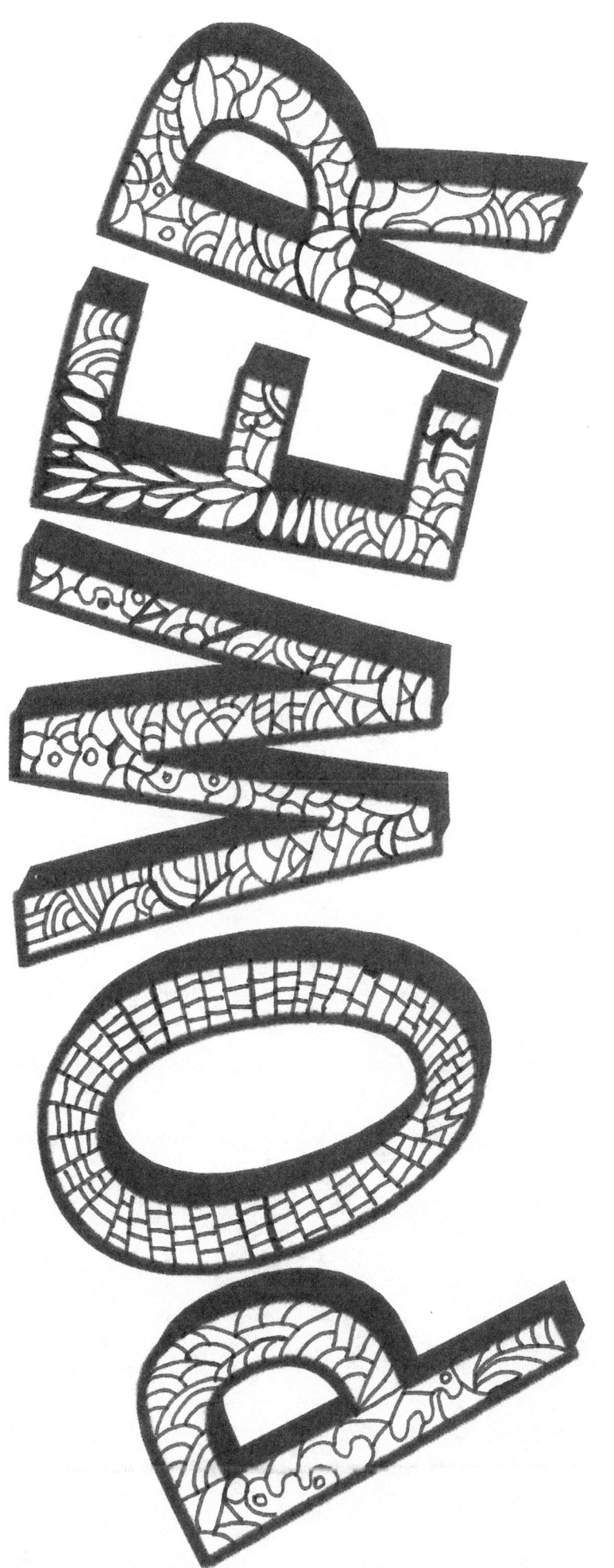

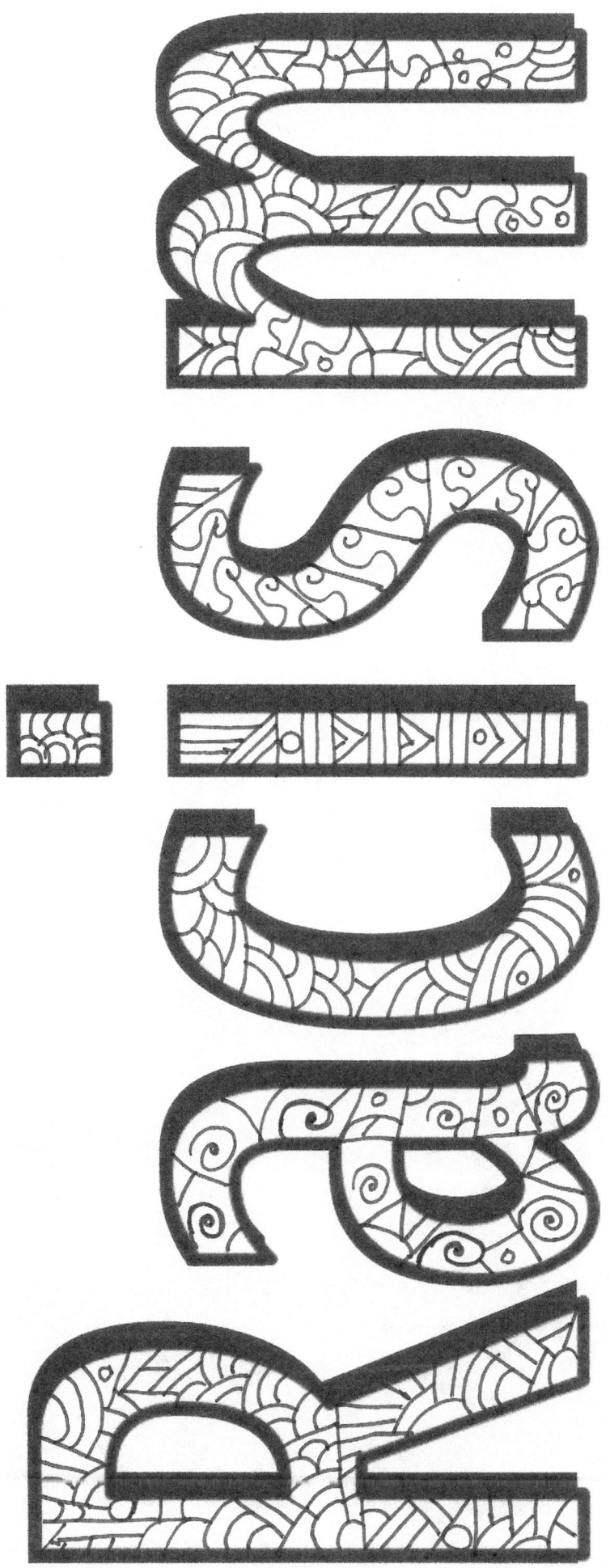

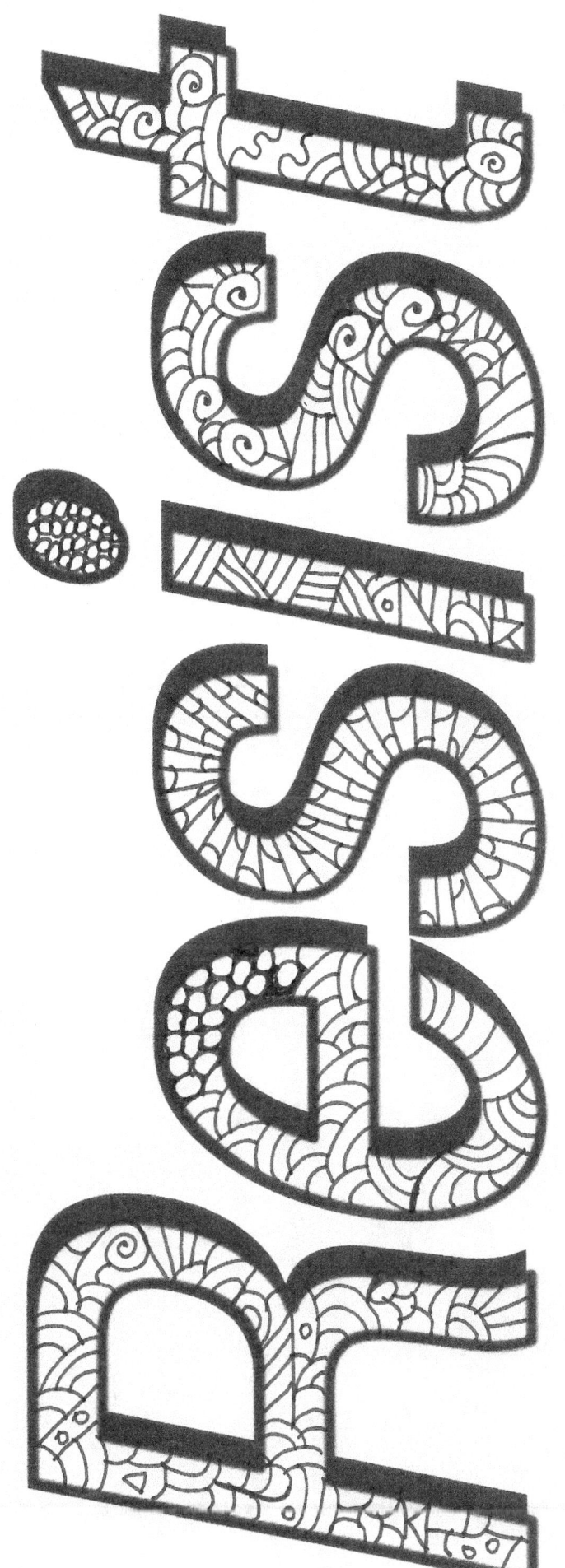

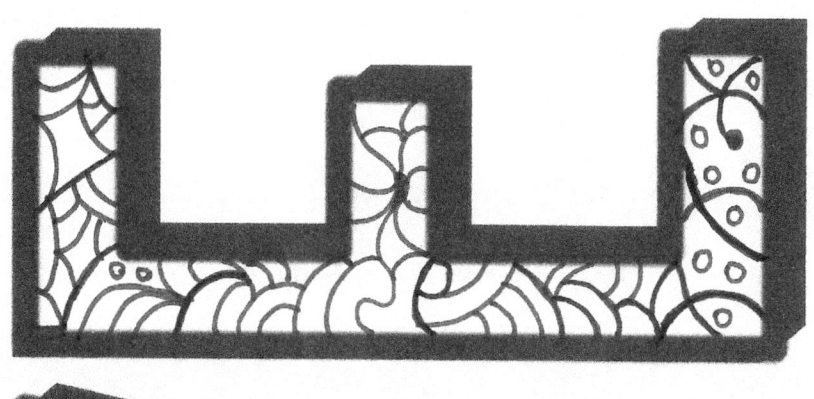
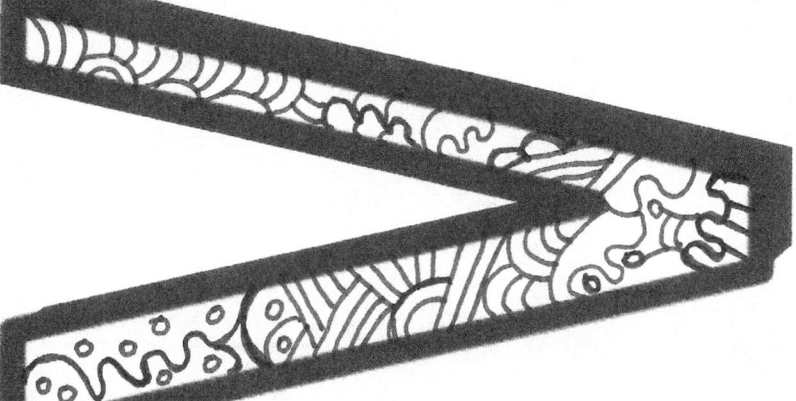
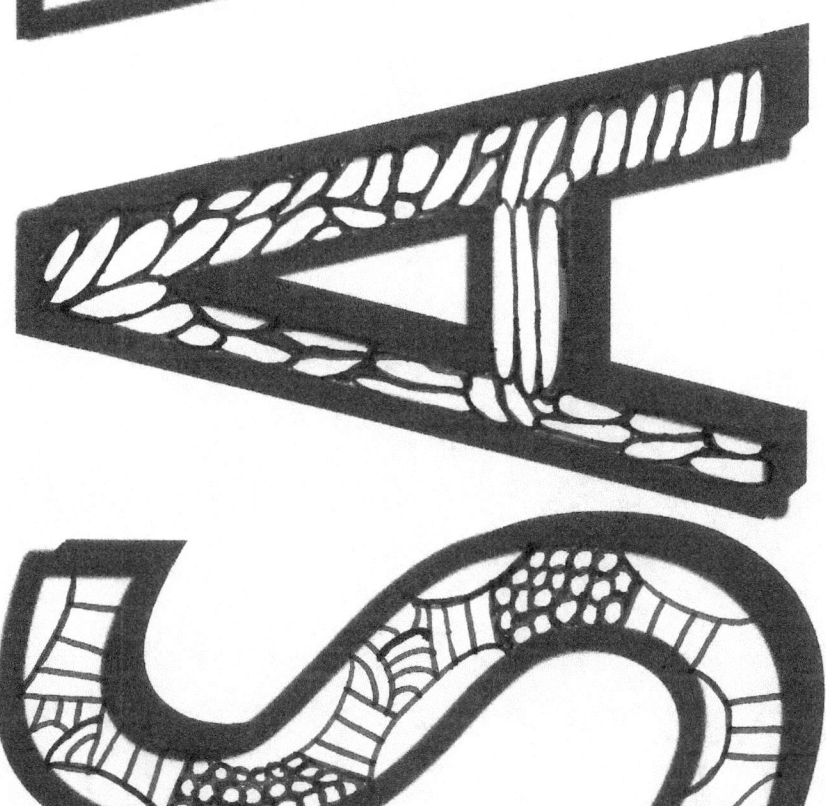

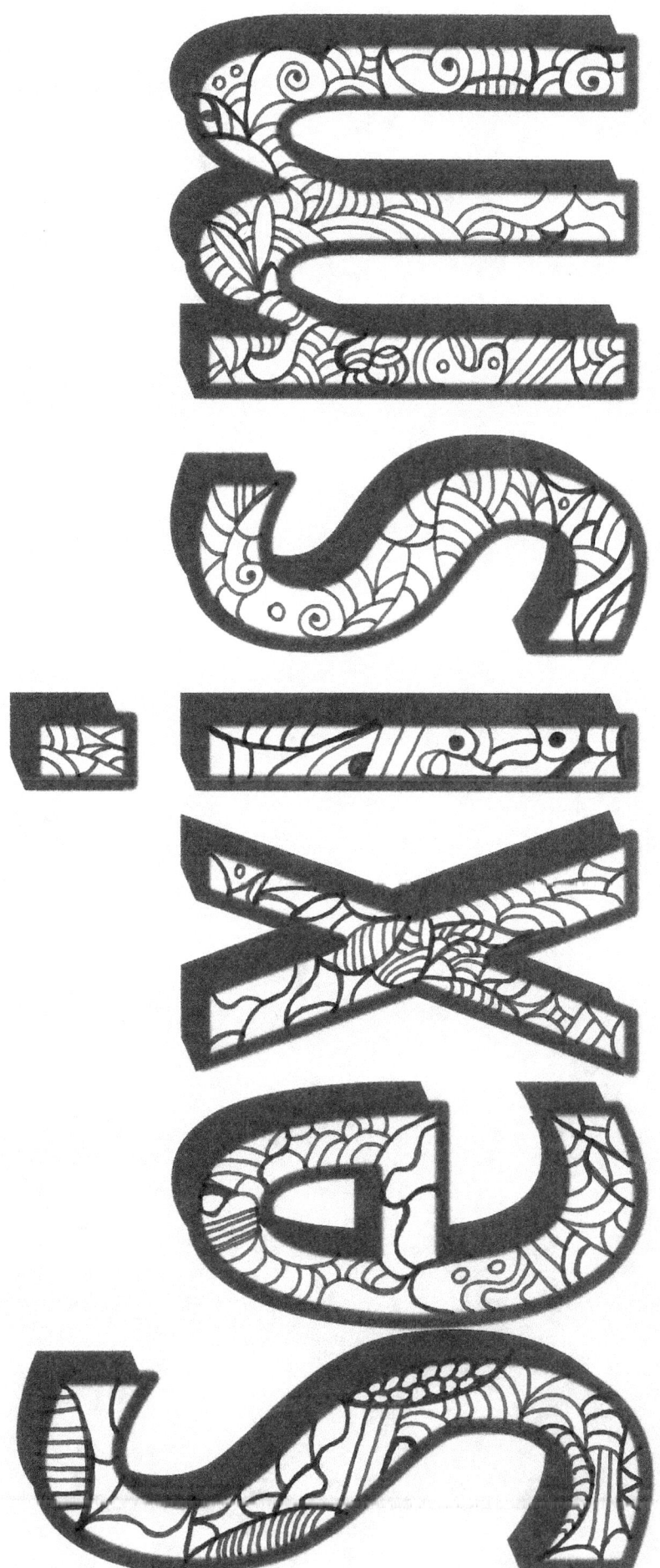

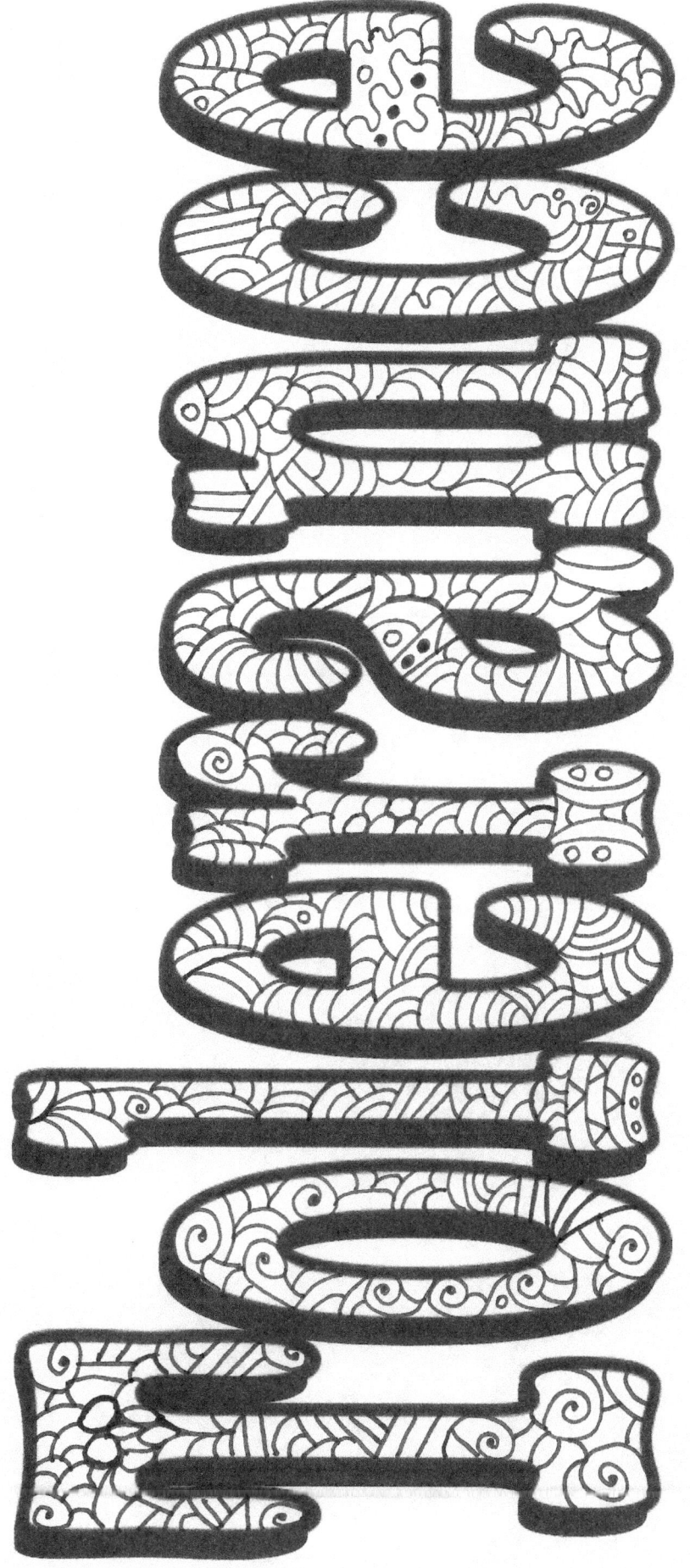

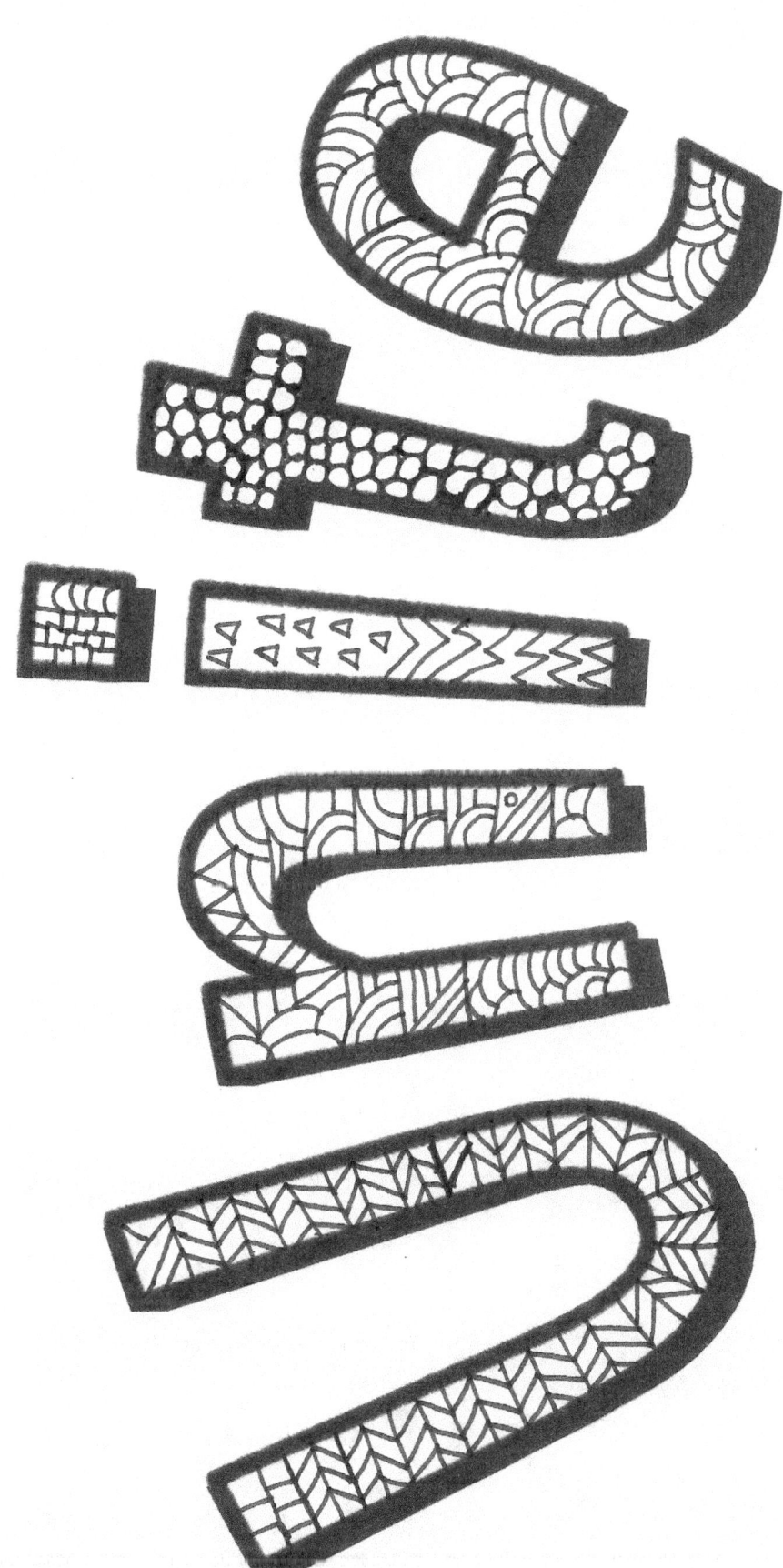

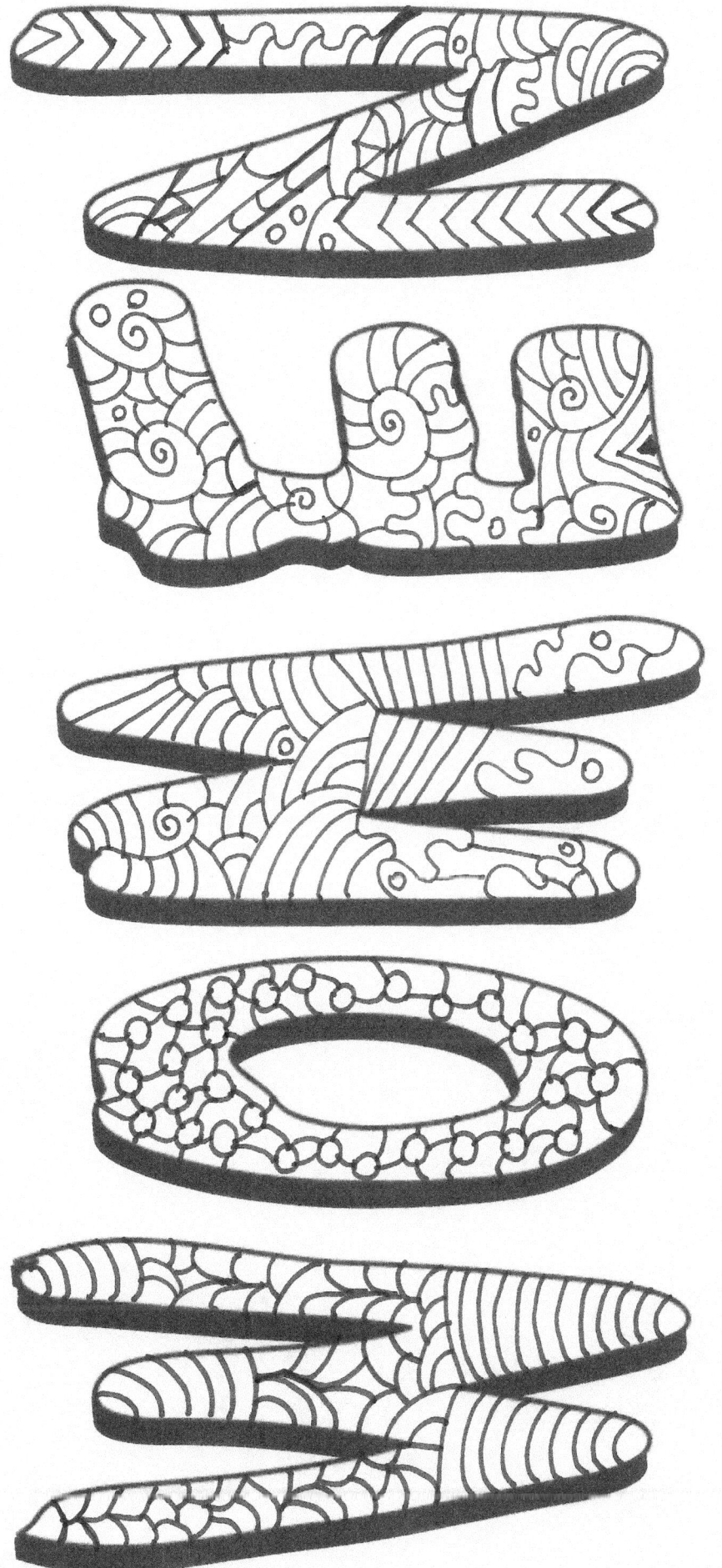

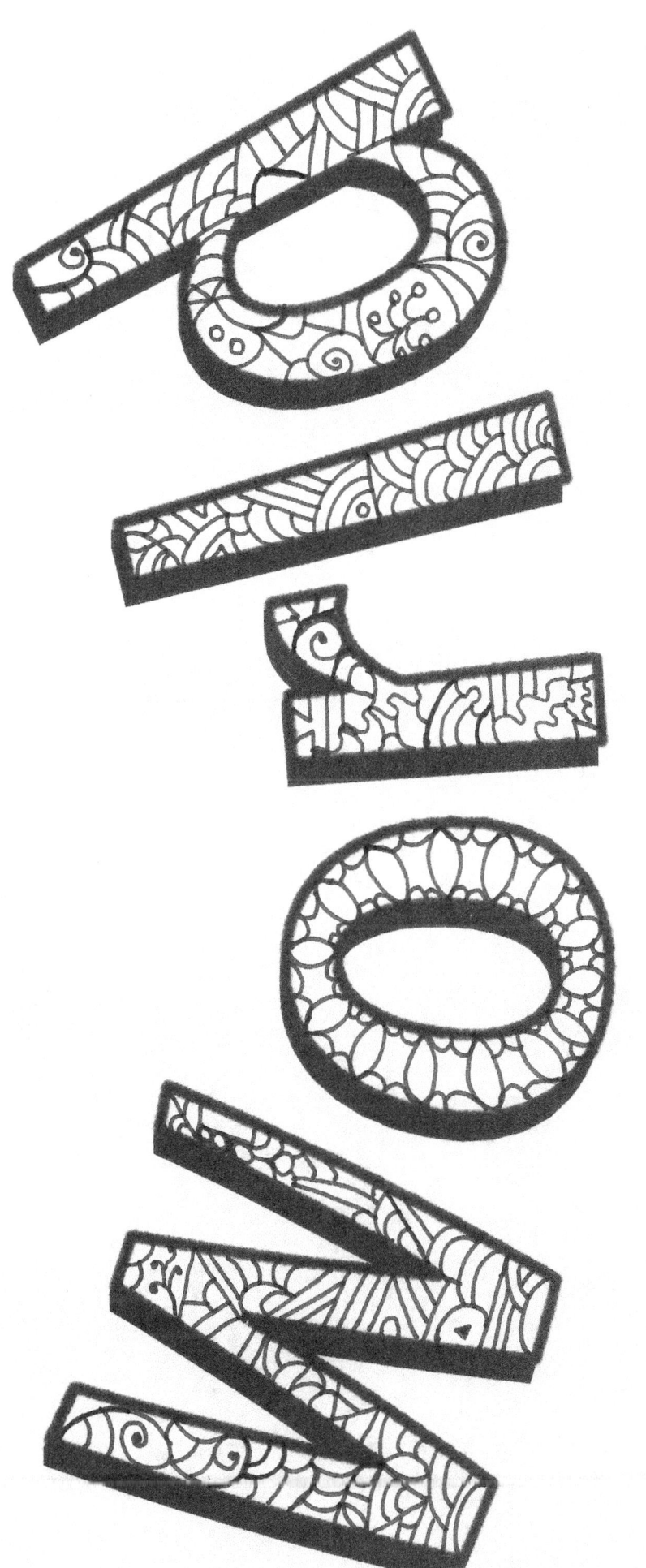

www.ingramcontent.com/pod-product-compliance
Lightning Source LLC
Chambersburg PA
CBHW081300180526
45170CB00007B/2502